contents

mornay sauce

When you add cheese to a white sauce it becomes mornay sauce, and is useful as a basis for many tasty dishes. Hard-boiled eggs, salmon, smoked fish, cooked chicken, asparagus and many different vegetables are some of the ingredients you can add to this kind of sauce. Here we have used it with tuna.

tuna mornay

preparation time 10 minutes
cooking time 25 minutes **serves** 2

30g butter
1 medium brown onion (150g), chopped finely
1 trimmed stick celery (75g), chopped finely
1 tablespoon plain flour
¾ cup (180ml) milk
½ cup (125ml) cream
⅓ cup (40g) grated cheddar cheese
130g can corn kernels, drained
185g can tuna, drained
½ cup (35g) stale breadcrumbs
¼ cup (30g) grated cheddar cheese, extra

1 Melt butter in medium saucepan; cook onion and celery, stirring constantly over medium heat, about 3 minutes or until onion is soft. Add flour; cook, stirring constantly, 1 minute or until mixture is bubbly. Gradually stir in combined milk and cream; stir constantly over high heat until mixture boils and thickens.
2 Remove from heat; add cheese, corn and tuna. Stir gently until cheese is melted. Spoon mixture into two 2-cup (500ml) ovenproof dishes. Sprinkle with combined breadcrumbs and extra cheese. Bake in moderate oven about 15 minutes or until heated through.

per serving 58.2g fat; 3480kJ (831 cal)
tips Milk can be used instead of the cream; we added cream for extra richness. Tuna mornay can be prepared up to the stage of baking a day ahead and refrigerated, covered.

microwave method
Combine butter, onion and celery in microwave-safe dish; cook on HIGH (100%) about 3 minutes or until onion is soft. Stir in flour, then milk and cream; cook on HIGH (100%) about 2 minutes or until mixture boils and thickens, stirring twice during cooking time. Stir in cheese, corn and tuna, sprinkle top with combined breadcrumbs and extra cheese; cook on HIGH (100%), uncovered, about 3 minutes or until cheese is melted.

Stirring in combined milk and cream

mornay fish pies

preparation time 25 minutes **cooking time** 35 minutes
serves 4

2½ cups (625ml) milk
½ small brown onion (40g)
1 bay leaf
6 black peppercorns
4 x 170g fish fillets, skinned
3 large potatoes (900g), chopped coarsely
600g celeriac, chopped coarsely
1 egg yolk
½ cup (40g) finely grated parmesan cheese
¾ cup (180ml) cream
60g butter
¼ cup (35g) plain flour
2 tablespoons coarsely chopped fresh flat-leaf parsley

1 Place milk, onion, bay leaf and peppercorns in large saucepan; bring to a boil. Add fish, reduce heat; simmer, covered, about 5 minutes or until cooked through. Remove fish from pan; divide fish among four 1½-cup (375ml) ovenproof dishes. Strain milk through sieve into medium jug. Discard solids; reserve milk.
2 Boil, steam or microwave potato and celeriac, separately, until tender; drain. Push potato and celeriac through sieve into large bowl; stir in yolk, cheese, ¼ cup of the cream and half of the butter until smooth. Cover to keep warm.
3 Meanwhile, melt remaining butter in medium saucepan; add flour, cook, stirring, about 3 minutes or until mixture bubbles and thickens slightly. Gradually stir in reserved milk and remaining cream; cook, stirring, until mixture boils and thickens. Stir in parsley.
4 Divide mornay mixture among dishes; cover with potato mixture. Place pies on baking tray; place under hot grill until browned lightly.

per serving 47.7g fat; 3478kJ (831 cal)

gnocchi with cheese sauce

preparation time 2 hours (plus refrigeration time) **cooking time** 40 minutes
serves 6

1.2kg potatoes, peeled
1 medium sweet potato (400g), peeled
300g spinach, trimmed, chopped coarsely
3 eggs
½ cup (40g) coarsely grated parmesan
2 cups (300g) plain flour
2 tablespoons olive oil
100g blue cheese, crumbled
⅓ cup (25g) finely grated pecorino

cheese sauce
30g butter
2 tablespoons plain flour
2½ cups (625ml) milk
⅔ cup (160ml) cream
½ cup (50g) finely grated gruyère
⅔ cup (50g) finely grated pecorino

1 Boil or steam potatoes until tender; drain and cool. Chop coarsely.
2 Meanwhile, microwave sweet potato on HIGH (100%) about 8 minutes until
tender; drain. Boil, steam or microwave spinach until wilted; drain.
3 Using wooden spoon, push potato through fine sieve. Divide mash among
three bowls; add one egg to each bowl; stir to combine. Using wooden spoon,
push sweet potato through fine sieve into one of the bowls; stir to combine.
Stir parmesan into second bowl and spinach into the third; stir to combine. Add
approximately ⅓ cup of flour to each bowl; stir each mixture to make a firm dough.
4 Roll each piece of dough on lightly floured surface into 2cm-thick sausage.
Cut each into 2cm pieces; roll into balls. Roll balls along the inside tines of a fork,
pressing lightly to form classic gnocchi shape – grooves on one side, dimple on
the other. Place in single layer on lightly floured trays, cover; refrigerate 1 hour.
5 Cook gnocchi, uncovered, in large pan of boiling water about 2 minutes until
gnocchi float to surface. Remove from pan; drain. Toss in large bowl with oil.
6 Make cheese sauce. Pour sauce over gnocchi; toss gently to coat. Place
gnocchi in lightly oiled large ovenproof dish; sprinkle with blue cheese then
pecorino. Place under hot grill about 3 minutes or until cheese browns lightly.

cheese sauce Melt butter in medium saucepan. Add flour; cook, stirring, until
mixture thickens and bubbles. Gradually add milk and cream; stir until mixture
boils and thickens. Remove from heat; stir in cheeses.

per serving 40.9g fat; 3313kJ (791 cal)

roast lamb with cauliflower cheese

preparation time 30 minutes **cooking time** 1 hour 10 minutes **serves** 6

2kg lamb leg
3 sprigs fresh rosemary, chopped coarsely
½ teaspoon sweet paprika
1kg potatoes, chopped coarsely
500g butternut squash, chopped coarsely
3 small brown onions (240g), halved
2 tablespoons olive oil
2 tablespoons plain flour
1 cup (250ml) chicken stock
¼ cup (60ml) dry red wine

cauliflower cheese
1 small cauliflower (1kg),
cut into florets
50g butter
¼ cup (35g) plain flour
2 cups (500ml) milk
¾ cup (90g) coarsely grated
cheddar cheese

1 Preheat oven to moderately hot.
2 Place lamb in large lightly oiled baking dish; using sharp knife, score skin at 2cm intervals, sprinkle with rosemary and paprika. Roast lamb, uncovered, in moderately hot oven 15 minutes. Reduce oven to moderate; roast lamb, uncovered, about 45 minutes or until cooked as desired.
3 Meanwhile, place potato, squash and onion, in single layer, in large shallow baking dish; drizzle with oil. Roast, uncovered, in moderate oven for last 45 minutes of lamb cooking time.
4 Make cauliflower cheese. Remove lamb and vegetables from oven; cover to keep warm. Strain pan juices from lamb into medium jug. Return ¼ cup of the pan juices to flameproof dish over medium heat, add flour; cook, stirring, about 5 minutes or until mixture bubbles and browns. Gradually add stock and wine; cook over high heat, stirring, until gravy boils and thickens.
5 Strain gravy; serve with sliced lamb, roast vegetables and cauliflower cheese.

cauliflower cheese Boil, steam or microwave cauliflower until tender; drain. Melt butter in medium saucepan, add flour; cook, stirring, until mixture bubbles and thickens. Gradually add milk; cook, stirring, until mixture boils and thickens. Stir in half of the cheese. Preheat grill. Place cauliflower in 1.5-litre (6-cup) shallow flameproof dish; pour sauce over cauliflower, sprinkle with remaining cheese. Place under preheated grill about 10 minutes or until browned lightly.

per serving 35.6g fat; 3244kJ (776 cal)

baked pasta & three cheese sauce

preparation time 10 minutes **cooking time** 30 minutes **serves** 4

375g macaroni pasta
300ml cream
⅓ cup (80ml) vegetable stock
1¼ cups (150g) grated mozzarella cheese
⅓ cup (75g) crumbled gorgonzola cheese
1¼ cups (100g) coarsely grated parmesan
1 teaspoon dijon mustard
2 tablespoons chopped fresh flat-leaf
    parsley
1 tablespoon chopped fresh chives

1 Preheat oven to moderate. Cook pasta in large saucepan of boiling water, uncovered, until just tender; drain.
2 Meanwhile, heat cream and stock in a saucepan until hot. Remove pan from heat, add mozzarella, gorgonzola and half the parmesan; stir until melted. Add mustard and herbs; season to taste with freshly ground black pepper. Add salt, if necessary. Combine cream mixture with drained pasta.
3 Pour cheesy pasta mixture into 2.5-litre (10-cup) ovenproof dish. Top with remaining parmesan. Bake, uncovered, 20 minutes or until browned.

per serving 59.2g fat; 3917kJ (937 cal)

lamb with mascarpone & white wine sauce

preparation time 10 minutes **cooking time** 15 minutes **serves** 4

¼ cup (60ml) olive oil
12 fresh sage leaves
100g sliced prosciutto
8 lamb steaks (640g)
1 clove garlic, crushed
¾ cup (180ml) dry white wine
½ cup (120g) mascarpone
¼ cup (60ml) cream

1 Heat oil in medium frying pan; cook sage until crisp. Drain on absorbent paper. Cook prosciutto, stirring, until crisp; drain on absorbent paper.
2 Cook lamb in same pan until browned both sides and cooked as desired. Remove from pan.
3 Cook garlic in same pan, stirring, until fragrant; add wine. Bring to a boil then reduce heat; simmer, uncovered, until liquid reduces by half. Add mascarpone and cream; cook, stirring, over heat until sauce boils and thickens slightly.
4 Divide lamb among serving plates; top with prosciutto and sage, drizzle with sauce. Serve with steamed asparagus, if desired.

per serving 49.9g fat; 2650kJ (633 cal)

spanish tortilla

preparation time 10 minutes cooking time 15 minutes
serves 4

1 tablespoon olive oil
1 large brown onion (200g), sliced thinly
750g canned tiny new potatoes, drained, sliced thickly
6 eggs, beaten lightly
100g feta cheese, chopped coarsely
⅓ cup (25g) finely grated parmesan cheese
⅓ cup (40g) coarsely grated cheddar cheese

1 Heat oil in medium frying pan; cook onion, stirring, until onion softens.
2 Combine onion, potato, egg and cheeses in large bowl.
3 Pour potato mixture into heated oiled medium non-stick frying pan. Cover; cook over low heat 10 minutes or until egg sets.
4 Carefully invert tortilla onto plate and slide back into frying pan. Cook further 5 minutes or until cooked through.
5 Remove from heat; allow to cool in pan. Serve with rocket salad, if desired.

per serving 23.8g fat; 1560kJ (373 cal)
tip Tortilla can be eaten hot or cold and makes great picnic fare.

omelette with ham & cheese

preparation time 5 minutes **cooking time** 5 minutes **serves** 1

2 eggs
1 tablespoon water
2 teaspoons butter
1 tablespoon finely chopped fresh chives
1 tablespoon small fresh basil leaves

filling
1 small tomato (130g), halved, deseeded
1 slice ham
¼ cup (30g) grated cheddar cheese

1 Break eggs into medium bowl; add the water. Use fork or whisk to mix only until yolks and whites are blended.
2 Heat 20cm frying pan over high heat for about 1 minute. Add butter to pan; it should sizzle and foam immediately if pan is hot enough. Do not allow butter to brown. Tip pan so butter covers base and halfway up side evenly.
3 Pour egg mixture into hot pan; it should begin to set around edge of pan almost immediately. Use wooden spoon to pull edge of omelette away from side of pan, allowing running mixture to reach hot pan and cook. Omelette is cooked when egg mixture no longer runs freely, but top still looks creamy. Omelette should be only browned lightly underneath.
4 Spoon filling over half of the omelette, opposite handle; this way, it is easier to slide omelette onto plate when cooked. Use egg slide to fold omelette in half, covering filling, and slide onto serving plate; serve omelette immediately, sprinkled with herbs.

filling Cut tomato flesh into strips. Cut ham into strips. Combine tomato and ham in bowl with cheese; mix lightly.

per serving 29.8g fat; 1628kJ (389 cal)

cheese & swiss chard pie

preparation time 40 minutes **cooking time** 50 minutes (plus cooling time)
serves 4

8 medium swiss chard leaves
30g butter
6 spring onions, chopped coarsely
½ cup (100g) cottage cheese
150g feta cheese, crumbled
⅓ cup (25g) grated parmesan cheese
¼ teaspoon ground nutmeg
4 eggs, beaten lightly
8 sheets fillo pastry
60g butter, melted, extra

1 Rinse swiss chard thoroughly under cold running water; trim away stems.
Place in large pan with just the water clinging to the leaves; cover. Bring to a boil;
reduce heat. Simmer, covered, about 3 minutes until tender. Pour into colander
or strainer to drain; cool to room temperature. Squeeze out as much excess
liquid as you can, using hands. Chop chard finely; place in medium bowl.
2 Heat butter in small frying pan; cook onion over medium heat about 3 minutes
or until onion is soft. Add to chard with cheeses, nutmeg and egg; stir well.
3 Place one pastry sheet on bench; brush with a little of the extra butter. Place
another layer on first sheet; brush with butter. Repeat layers with two more sheets
of pastry and butter.
4 Grease 13cm x 23cm ovenproof dish. Place the four joined sheets carefully
into dish; trim pastry, using scissors, about 2cm from the edge of dish. Spread
chard mixture evenly into dish, do not press down.
5 Layer remaining four pastry sheets with some of the remaining butter; fold
pastry in half. Lightly moisten edges of pastry in dish with water; place folded
pastry on top of filling, trim edges of pastry, brush top with remaining butter.
6 Bake in moderately hot oven about 40 minutes or until golden brown. Serve
topped with spring onion and parsley, if desired.

per serving 37.1g fat; 2124kJ (507 cal)
tips Recipe is best made just before serving. Pie can be served hot or cold.

chicken enchiladas

preparation time 50 minutes **cooking time** 35 minutes **serves** 10

3 chipotle chillies
1 cup (250ml) boiling water
500g chicken breast fillets
1 tablespoon vegetable oil
1 large red onion (300g), chopped finely
2 cloves garlic, crushed
1 teaspoon ground cumin

1 tablespoon tomato paste
2 x 425g cans crushed tomatoes
1 tablespoon finely chopped oregano
⅔ cup (160g) soured cream
1½ cups (240g) coarsely grated
   cheddar cheese
10 small flour tortillas

1 Cover chillies with the water in small heatproof bowl; stand 20 minutes. Remove stems from chillies; discard stems. Blend or process chillies with soaking liquid until smooth.
2 Meanwhile, place chicken in medium saucepan of boiling water; return to a boil. Reduce heat; simmer, covered, about 10 minutes or until chicken is cooked through. Remove chicken from poaching liquid; cool 10 minutes. Discard poaching liquid (or keep for another use); shred chicken finely.
3 Preheat oven to moderate. Lightly oil a shallow rectangular 3-litre (12-cup) ovenproof dish.
4 Heat oil in large frying pan; cook onion, stirring, until soft. Reserve half of the onion in small bowl.
5 Add garlic and cumin to remaining onion in pan; cook, stirring, until fragrant. Add chilli mixture, tomato paste, undrained tomatoes and oregano; bring to a boil. Reduce heat; simmer, uncovered, 1 minute. Remove sauce from heat.
6 Meanwhile, combine shredded chicken, reserved onion, half of the soured cream and a third of the cheese in medium bowl.
7 Warm tortillas according to instructions on packet. Dip tortillas, one at a time, in tomato sauce in pan; place on board. Place ¼ cup of the chicken mixture along edge of each tortilla; roll enchiladas to enclose filling.
8 Spread ½ cup tomato sauce into prepared dish. Place enchiladas, seam-side down, in dish (they should fit snugly, without overcrowding). Pour remaining tomato sauce over enchiladas; sprinkle with remaining cheese. Cook, uncovered, about 15 minutes or until cheese melts and enchiladas are heated through. Serve with remaining soured cream.

per serving 9.4g fat; 1593kJ (381 cal)

cheese scones

preparation time 10 minutes cooking time 20 minutes serves 12

1 cup self-raising flour
pinch cayenne pepper
2 tablespoons finely grated
parmesan cheese
½ cup coarsely grated cheddar
cheese
½ cup milk

1 Preheat oven to hot. Lightly
grease and flour 8cm x 26cm
baking tin.
2 Combine flour, cayenne,
parmesan and half the cheddar in
medium bowl; pour in milk, stir until
mixture forms a sticky dough.
Gently knead dough on floured
surface until smooth; use hand to
flatten dough to 2cm-thickness.
3 Using 4.5cm cutter, cut rounds
from dough; place rounds, slightly
touching, in tin. Brush scones with
a little milk then sprinkle with
remaining cheddar. Bake about
20 minutes.

per serving 7.8g fat; 907kJ
(217 cal)
tip These scones make a delicious
accompaniment with soup.

mini cheese muffins

preparation time 10 minutes **cooking time** 25 minutes **makes** 12

3 cups (450g) self-raising flour
40g butter, chopped coarsely
1¾ cups (430ml) buttermilk
2 tablespoons basil pesto
¾ cup (90g) coarsely grated cheddar cheese
¼ teaspoon sweet paprika
1 tablespoon plain flour

1 Preheat oven to moderately hot. Grease 12-hole mini muffin tray.
2 Place self-raising flour in large bowl; rub in butter with fingertips. Stir in buttermilk with fork to form a soft, sticky dough. Swirl in pesto and cheese; do not overmix.
3 Divide mixture among holes of prepared tray. Sprinkle with combined paprika and plain flour. Bake in moderately hot oven 25 minutes.
4 Stand muffins in tray 5 minutes before turning out onto wire rack.

per muffin 7.8g fat; 929kJ (222 cal)

beef salad with blue-cheese dressing

preparation time 10 minutes (plus standing time)
cooking time 20 minutes **serves** 4

500g tiny new potatoes, quartered
1 tablespoon olive oil
4 fillet steaks (500g)
300g green beans, trimmed, halved crossways
200g baby plum tomatoes, halved
100g baby rocket leaves

blue-cheese dressing
¼ cup (60ml) olive oil
2 cloves garlic, crushed
¼ cup (60ml) orange juice
60g blue cheese, crumbled

1 Preheat oven to very hot.
2 Place potato, in single layer, in large shallow baking dish; drizzle with oil. Roast, uncovered, in very hot oven about 20 minutes or until lightly browned and tender.
3 Make blue-cheese dressing.
4 Cook steaks on heated oiled grill plate (or grill or barbecue) until browned both sides and cooked as desired. Cover; stand 5 minutes.
5 Meanwhile, boil, steam or microwave beans until just tender; drain well.
6 Slice steak thinly. Combine steak, beans and potato in large bowl with tomato and rocket, drizzle with blue-cheese dressing; toss gently to combine.

blue-cheese dressing Combine ingredients in screw-top jar; shake well.

per serving 31.9g fat; 2143kJ (512 cal)

cheese & spinach tortellini with gorgonzola sauce

preparation time 5 minutes **cooking time** 15 minutes
serves 4

30g butter
2 tablespoons plain flour
1 cup (250ml) milk
¾ cup (180ml) cream
100g gorgonzola cheese, chopped coarsely
750g cheese and spinach tortellini
¼ cup loosely packed fresh flat-leaf parsley
freshly ground black pepper

1 Melt butter in medium saucepan; cook flour, stirring, about
2 minutes or until mixture bubbles and thickens.
2 Gradually stir in milk and cream; bring to a boil. Reduce heat;
simmer, uncovered, until sauce boils and thickens. Remove from
heat; stir in cheese.
3 Meanwhile, cook pasta in large saucepan of boiling water,
uncovered, until just tender; drain.
4 Combine pasta with sauce; sprinkle with parsley and pepper.

per serving 43.8g fat; 3017kJ (721 cal)
tips Ravioli or gnocchi can be substituted for the tortellini.
It's best to choose a ricotta and spinach filled tortellini (or the
even simpler ricotta filled version) when making this sauce, as it
doesn't marry overly well with meat-filled pastas.

gorgonzola fritters

preparation time 15 minutes (plus standing time) **cooking time** 5 minutes
makes 36

1 cup (200g) ricotta cheese
1 cup (185g) gorgonzola cheese, chopped coarsely
2 eggs, beaten lightly
½ cup (75g) plain flour
vegetable oil for deep-frying
1 cup (80g) finely grated parmesan cheese

1 Combine ricotta, gorgonzola and egg in medium bowl. Whisk in flour;
stand at room temperature 1 hour.
2 Heat oil in large saucepan; deep-fry heaped teaspoons of mixture, turning
occasionally, until fritters are lightly browned all over and cooked through.
Do not have oil too hot or fritters will over-brown before cooking through.
Place parmesan in bowl; toss fritters, in batches, to coat as they are cooked.

per serving 4g fat; 231kJ (55 cal)

blue cheese & caramelised leek tartlets

preparation time 25 minutes
cooking time 40 minutes
makes 24

20g butter
1 tablespoon olive oil
8 cloves garlic, peeled, halved
   lengthways
1 large leek (500g), sliced thinly
2 teaspoons brown sugar
1 sheet ready-rolled puff pastry
60g blue cheese, crumbled

1 Heat butter and oil in large frying pan; add garlic, cook, stirring, over very low heat, about 10 minutes or until soft and browned lightly. Remove from pan.

2 Add leek to pan; cook, stirring, until soft. Add sugar; cook, stirring occasionally, about 15 minutes or until mixture caramelises. Preheat oven to hot.

3 Cut rounds from pastry sheet using 4.5cm cutter. Place rounds on greased oven tray. Grease underside of another oven tray; place greased side on top of pastry (this stops it from rising). Bake rounds in hot oven about 10 minutes or until browned lightly. Remove top oven tray.

4 Divide cheese among rounds; top with caramelised leek and piece of garlic. Return tarts to oven for further 5 minutes or until cheese is soft. Serve warm.

per tartlet 3.9g fat; 222kJ (53 cal)

camembert with pear compote on pumpernickel bites

preparation time 20 minutes (plus cooling time) **cooking time** 10 minutes **makes** 24

½ cup (75g) dried pears, chopped finely
2 tablespoons dried cranberries, chopped finely
1 cinnamon stick
1 tablespoon caster sugar
¼ cup (60ml) water
200g whole camembert
24 cocktail pumpernickel rounds (250g)
1 tablespoon toasted pistachios, chopped finely

1 Combine pear, craisins, cinnamon, sugar and the water in small saucepan; bring to a boil. Reduce heat; simmer, uncovered, 10 minutes. Cool to room temperature. Discard cinnamon.
2 Cut cheese into 24 wedges.
3 Place rounds on serving platter; top each round with a wedge of cheese, ½ teaspoon of the compote then a sprinkle of nuts.

per piece 2.6g fat; 268kJ (64 cal)

tagliatelle with
brie & mushrooms

preparation time 15 minutes **cooking time** 25 minutes
serves 4

400g tagliatelle
200g brie, chilled
60g butter
6 spring onions, chopped finely
2 cloves garlic, crushed
300g button mushrooms, sliced thinly
200g flat mushrooms, sliced thinly
½ cup (125ml) dry white wine
1 cup (250ml) vegetable stock
1 tablespoon wholegrain mustard
¼ cup (25g) drained sun-dried tomatoes, sliced thinly
1 cup (250ml) cream
2 teaspoons finely chopped fresh thyme

1 Cook pasta in large saucepan of boiling water; boil,
uncovered, until just tender.
2 Meanwhile, remove rind from cheese; slice cheese thinly.
3 Heat butter in large saucepan; cook onion, garlic and
mushrooms, stirring, until mushrooms are soft.
4 Add wine and stock; simmer, uncovered, until liquid reduces
by half.
5 Add mustard, tomato, cheese, cream and thyme; stir until
cheese melts. Drain pasta; serve with sauce.

per serving 58.3g fat; 4081kJ (975 cal)

feta, spinach & prosciutto lamb rolls with herbed potatoes

preparation time 20 minutes **cooking time** 20 minutes
serves 4

500g salad potatoes, halved lengthways
20g butter
1 tablespoon finely chopped fresh flat-leaf parsley
12 slices prosciutto (180g)
20g baby spinach leaves
160g feta cheese, sliced thinly
4 x 200g pieces lamb fillet
1 tablespoon olive oil

1 Boil, steam or microwave potato until tender; drain. Toss in
large bowl with butter and parsley; cover to keep warm.
2 Meanwhile, slightly overlap three slices of the prosciutto, side
by side, on board; layer with a quarter of the spinach, a quarter
of the cheese and one piece of the lamb. Starting from narrow
end of prosciutto slices, roll carefully to completely enclose lamb.
Repeat with remaining prosciutto, spinach, cheese and lamb.
3 Heat oil in large frying pan; cook lamb rolls about 15 minutes
or until browned all over and cooked as desired. Cover lamb;
stand 10 minutes. Serve lamb sliced thickly with herbed potato
and, if desired, a salad of mixed baby leaves.

per serving 38.3g fat; 2725kJ (652 cal)

greek cheese & prawn ravioli

preparation time 50 minutes **cooking time** 20 minutes
serves 4

¼ cup (60ml) extra virgin olive oil
5 large tomatoes (1.2kg), deseeded, chopped coarsely
4 cloves garlic, crushed
¼ cup finely chopped fresh lemon thyme
700g uncooked medium prawns
⅓ cup (80g) soured cream
1 teaspoon finely grated lemon rind
200g feta, crumbled
40 wonton wrappers

1 Heat 2 tablespoons of the oil in large saucepan; cook tomato,
garlic and 2 tablespoons of the thyme, stirring, 2 minutes.
Cover; cook over low heat for 5 minutes.
2 Meanwhile, shell and devein prawns; chop prawn meat
coarsely. Combine prawn meat in medium bowl with soured
cream, rind, 150g of the cheese and remaining thyme.
3 Centre a level tablespoon of the prawn mixture on one wonton
wrapper; brush around edges with water. Top with another
wrapper, press edges together to seal. Repeat with remaining
wrappers and filling; you will have 20 ravioli.
4 Cook ravioli, in two batches, in large saucepan of boiling
water, uncovered, until ravioli float to the surface and are cooked
through. Drain; divide ravioli among serving plates, top with hot
tomato mixture, sprinkle with remaining cheese then drizzle with
remaining oil. Top with extra thyme, if desired.

per serving 35g fat; 2261kJ (540 cal)

hot spinach cheesecake

preparation time 25 minutes (plus refrigeration time)
cooking time 1 hour 20 minutes **serves** 8

60g butter
1 cup (100g) finely crushed cheese biscuit crumbs
¼ cup (20g) grated parmesan cheese

spinach filling
600g spinach, trimmed
1 medium brown onion (150g), chopped finely
250g cream cheese
125g feta cheese
1 cup (250ml) soured cream
4 eggs, beaten lightly

1 Melt butter in medium saucepan. Add biscuit crumbs; mix
well. Press evenly over base of greased 20cm springform cake
tin; refrigerate, covered, 30 minutes.
2 Make spinach filling.
3 Stand biscuit base on baking tray and pour spinach filling over.
Bake, uncovered, in moderately low oven about 1¼ hours or until
golden brown and set. Sprinkle with parmesan; stand 10 minutes
before cutting.

spinach filling Boil, steam or microwave spinach until just
tender; drain. Press excess liquid from spinach; chop spinach
coarsely. Cook onion in small frying pan, stirring constantly, until
onion is soft. Beat cheeses in small bowl with electric mixer until
smooth. Add soured cream and egg; beat until combined.
Transfer to large bowl; stir in spinach and onion.

per serving 38.5g fat; 1827kJ (36 cal)
tip Sprinkle with chopped cooked bacon rashers before baking,
if you prefer.

chicken breast with smoked salmon & goat's cheese stuffing

preparation time 25 minutes **cooking time** 1 hour 15 minutes **serves** 4

4 medium potatoes (800g), sliced thinly
¼ cup coarsely chopped fresh flat-leaf parsley
2 cloves garlic, crushed
1 tablespoon olive oil
⅔ cup (160ml) milk, warmed
2 tablespoons finely chopped fresh chives
100g soft goat's cheese
4 breast fillets (800g)
4 slices smoked salmon (120g)
50g baby spinach leaves

spinach salad
100g baby spinach leaves
1 tablespoon olive oil
2 tablespoons lemon juice
1 clove garlic, crushed

1 Preheat oven to moderately hot (200°C/180°C fan-assisted).
2 Combine potato, parsley, garlic and oil in medium bowl. Layer potato mixture in 2.5-litre (10-cup) ceramic baking dish; pour over milk. Roast, uncovered, about 40 minutes or until potato is just tender.
3 Meanwhile, combine chives and cheese in small bowl. Cut fillets in half horizontally almost all the way through; open out each fillet. Spread each fillet with a quarter of the cheese mixture; top with one slice of salmon and a quarter of the spinach. Roll each fillet tightly to enclose filling; secure with toothpicks.
4 Cook chicken in large oiled frying pan, uncovered, until browned.
5 Place chicken on cooked potato; roast, uncovered, about 15 minutes or until chicken is cooked through. Stand 5 minutes; remove toothpicks, slice thickly.
6 Meanwhile, place ingredients for spinach salad in medium bowl; toss gently to combine. Serve chicken with potato and salad.

per serving 21g fat; 2316kJ (554 cal)

goat's cheese soufflé with creamed spinach sauce

preparation time 15 minutes **cooking time** 25 minutes (plus cooling time)
serves 6

cooking-oil spray
¼ cup (25g) packaged breadcrumbs
30g butter
2 tablespoons plain flour
1 cup (250ml) milk
4 eggs, separated
¼ teaspoon cayenne pepper
150g firm goat's cheese, crumbled

creamed spinach sauce
180g baby spinach leaves
⅔ cup (160ml) cream, warmed

1 Preheat oven to moderately hot. Spray six 1-cup (250ml) soufflé dishes with cooking-oil spray, sprinkle with breadcrumbs; place on baking tray.
2 Melt butter in small saucepan, add flour; cook, stirring, until mixture bubbles and thickens. Gradually add milk; stir until mixture boils and thickens. Transfer to large bowl; stir in egg yolks, pepper and cheese; cool 5 minutes.
3 Beat egg whites in small bowl with electric mixer until soft peaks form; gently fold whites, in two batches, into cheese mixture.
4 Divide mixture among prepared dishes; bake, uncovered, about 15 minutes or until soufflés are puffed and browned lightly.
5 Meanwhile, make creamed spinach sauce. Serve soufflés with sauce.

creamed spinach sauce Boil, steam or microwave spinach until just wilted; drain. Using hand, squeeze out excess liquid. Blend or process spinach until almost smooth. With motor operating, gradually add cream; process until smooth.

per serving 26.1g fat; 1304kJ (312 cal)

haloumi & lamb kebabs

preparation time 20 minutes **cooking time** 20 minutes **makes** 8 kebabs

½ teaspoon ground allspice
1 teaspoon cracked black pepper
1 clove garlic, crushed
2 tablespoons lemon juice
2 tablespoons olive oil
500g diced lamb
200g haloumi cheese, diced into 2cm pieces

1 Place allspice, pepper, garlic, juice and oil in medium bowl; add lamb, turn to coat in mixture. Thread lamb and cheese, alternately, onto skewers.
2 Cook kebabs on heated oiled grill plate (or grill or barbecue) until browned all over and cooked as desired.

per serving 28.7g fat; 1710kJ (409 cal)

mediterranean haloumi bruschetta

preparation time 15 minutes **cooking time** 10 minutes **serves** 4

1 small french breadstick
1 tablespoon olive oil
1 small aubergine (230g), sliced thinly
200g haloumi cheese, sliced thinly
2 tablespoons plain flour
2 medium plum tomatoes (150g), sliced thinly
2 tablespoons fresh baby basil leaves
1 tablespoon baby capers, rinsed, drained

1 Preheat oven to hot.
2 Cut bread, on an angle, into eight slices; brush both sides with half of the oil, place on oven tray. Toast, uncovered, about 5 minutes.
3 Meanwhile, cook aubergine on heated oiled grill plate (or grill or barbecue) until just tender.
4 Coat haloumi in flour; cook on heated oiled grill plate (or grill or barbecue) until browned lightly.
5 Divide aubergine, haloumi, tomatoes, basil and capers evenly among bruschetta. Drizzle with remaining oil.

per serving 14.6g fat; 1204kJ (288 cal)

aubergine & haloumi skewers with roasted tomato sauce

preparation time 35 minutes **cooking time** 20 minutes (plus cooling time) **makes** 36 skewers

1 medium aubergine (300g)
250g haloumi cheese
¼ cup (35g) plain flour
1 egg, beaten lightly
½ cup (35g) fresh breadcrumbs
½ cup (40g) finely grated parmesan
36 medium fresh basil leaves
vegetable oil, for deep-frying

roasted tomato sauce
125g cherry tomatoes
cooking-oil spray
1 clove garlic, crushed
½ teaspoon white sugar
1 teaspoon red wine vinegar
1 tablespoon olive oil
36 toothpicks

1 Make roasted tomato sauce.
2 Meanwhile, cut aubergine into 36 squares. Cut haloumi into 36 squares.
3 Coat aubergine squares in flour, shake off excess; dip into egg then coat in combined breadcrumbs and parmesan.
4 Thread one piece of aubergine, one basil leaf and one piece of haloumi onto each toothpick. Heat oil in wok, deep-fry skewers, in batches, about 30 seconds or until browned lightly; drain on absorbent paper.
5 Serve with roasted tomato sauce.

roasted tomato sauce Preheat oven to moderate (180°C/160°C fan-assisted). Line baking tray with baking parchment. Place tomatoes on prepared tray; spray with oil. Roast, uncovered, about 15 minutes or until soft. Blend or process tomatoes with remaining ingredients until smooth. Cool to room temperature.

per skewer 3.4g fat; 196kJ (47 cal)

sicilian stuffed pizza

preparation time 20 minutes **cooking time** 35 minutes (plus standing time)
serves 4

¾ cup (180ml) warm water
1½ teaspoons (7g) dried yeast
½ teaspoon sugar
2 cups (300g) plain flour
1 teaspoon salt
⅓ cup (80ml) olive oil
1 cup (70g) stale breadcrumbs
2 cloves garlic, crushed
1 teaspoon ground fennel

1 small red onion (100g), chopped
  finely
250g minced beef
100g Italian salami, chopped finely
425g can crushed tomatoes
¼ cup (40g) pine nuts, toasted
¼ cup chopped fresh flat-leaf parsley
½ cup (50g) finely grated mozzarella
  cheese

1 Combine the water, yeast and sugar in small bowl, cover; stand in warm
place about 15 minutes or until frothy. Combine flour and salt in large bowl, stir in
yeast mixture and half of the oil; mix to a soft dough. Turn dough onto lightly
floured surface, knead about 5 minutes or until smooth and elastic. Place dough
in large lightly oiled bowl, cover; stand in warm place about 1 hour or until dough
doubles in size.
2 Meanwhile, heat remaining oil in large frying pan; cook breadcrumbs and half
of the garlic, stirring, until crumbs are browned lightly. Remove from pan.
3 Reheat same pan; cook fennel, onion and remaining garlic, stirring, until onion
just softens. Add mince; cook, stirring, until mince changes colour. Stir in salami
and undrained tomatoes; bring to a boil. Reduce heat; simmer, uncovered,
stirring occasionally, about 15 minutes or until liquid reduces by half. Remove
from heat; stir in nuts and parsley. Cool.
4 Preheat oven to hot.
5 Knead dough on lightly floured surface until smooth; divide in half. Roll each
half into 30cm round. Place one round on lightly oiled pizza or oven tray, top with
breadcrumb mixture, mince mixture, cheese then remaining round. Pinch edges
together; bake, uncovered, in hot oven about 15 minutes or until browned lightly.
6 Stand pizza 10 minutes before cutting into wedges and serving with a rocket
and parmesan salad, if desired.

per serving 47.7g fat; 3610kJ (862 cal)

pesto, mozzarella & artichoke pizza

preparation time 10 minutes cooking time 25 minutes serves 4

30cm homemade or purchased pizza base
190g jar pesto
100g marinated aubergine slices
200g char-grilled pepper slices
2 drained marinated artichoke hearts, sliced thickly
200g mozzarella, sliced thickly
2 tablespoons pine nuts

1 Place pizza base on oiled baking tray. Spread pesto over base; top with aubergine, pepper and artichokes. Arrange cheese on top; sprinkle with pine nuts.
2 Bake, uncovered, in moderately hot oven about 20 minutes or until base is cooked through and cheese is bubbling.

per serving 40.1g fat; 2581kJ (616 cal)

aubergine & mozzarella slices

preparation time 15 minutes cooking time 15 minutes serves 8

2 medium aubergines (600g), peeled
250g mozzarella cheese
8 large basil leaves
¼ cup (60ml) olive oil

1 Cut aubergine into 2cm-thick rounds (you will need eight rounds). Split each round in half, horizontally, taking care not to cut all the way through. Gently open out rounds.
2 Cut cheese into eight slices. Place cheese in each of the aubergine rounds. Place one basil leaf on each piece of cheese. Fold over aubergine; trim cheese to size of aubergine if necessary.
3 Heat oil in medium non-stick frying pan. Cook aubergine over medium heat until browned both sides and tender and cheese begins to melt.

per serving 13.9g fat; 701kJ (167 cal)

cheese & spinach quesadillas

preparation time 20 minutes **cooking time** 10 minutes
serves 8

⅔ cup (130g) low-fat cottage cheese
100g spinach leaves, trimmed
1 medium avocado (250g), chopped finely
1 cup (200g) canned mexican-style beans, drained
125g can corn kernels, drained
2 medium tomatoes (380g), deseeded, chopped finely
1 small red onion (100g), chopped finely
2 medium courgettes (240g), grated coarsely
16 small flour tortillas
1½ cups (150g) coarsely grated low-fat mozzarella

1 Blend or process cottage cheese and spinach until smooth.
Combine avocado, beans, corn, tomato, onion and courgettes
in medium bowl.
2 Place eight tortillas on lightly oiled oven tray; divide spinach
mixture among tortillas, leaving 2cm border around edge.
Divide avocado mixture among tortillas, sprinkling it over spinach
mixture. Top each with one of the remaining tortillas.
3 Sprinkle mozzarella over quesadilla stacks; place under
preheated grill until cheese just melts and browns lightly.

per serving 11.8g fat; 1177kJ (282 cal)
tips Quesadillas are filled tortillas which are grilled or fried and
served with fresh salsa. We used small flour tortillas measuring
approximately 16cm in diameter; they are sometimes labelled
'fajita tortillas' on the package.

soupe au pistou

preparation time 15 minutes (plus soaking time) **cooking time** 1 hour 40 minutes **serves** 8

1 cup (200g) dried cannellini beans
⅓ cup (80ml) olive oil
2 veal shanks (1.5kg), trimmed
1 large leek (500g), sliced thinly
2 litres (8 cups) water
2 cups (500ml) chicken stock
2 tablespoons toasted pine nuts
1 clove garlic, quartered
¼ cup (20g) finely grated parmesan cheese
½ cup firmly packed fresh basil leaves
2 medium carrots (240g), chopped coarsely
200g green beans, trimmed, chopped coarsely

1 Cover cannellini beans with cold water in large bowl; stand, covered, overnight.
2 Heat 1 tablespoon of the oil in large saucepan; cook shanks, uncovered, until browned all over. Remove from pan. Cook leek in same pan, stirring, about 5 minutes or until just softened. Return shanks to pan with the water and stock; bring to a boil. Reduce heat; simmer, covered, 1 hour.
3 Meanwhile, blend or process remaining oil, nuts, garlic and cheese until combined. Add basil; process until pistou mixture forms a paste.
4 Remove shanks from soup. When cool enough to handle, remove meat from bones. Discard bones; chop meat coarsely. Return meat to soup with rinsed and drained cannellini beans; bring to a boil. Reduce heat; simmer, uncovered, 20 minutes. Add carrot; simmer, uncovered, 10 minutes. Add green beans and pistou; simmer, uncovered, 5 minutes.
5 Divide soup among serving bowls. Serve with slices of warm baguette, if desired, for dipping in soup.

per serving 15g fat; 1265kJ (302 cal)

parmesan crisps

preparation time 5 minutes **cooking time** 25 minutes **makes** 18

1 cup (80g) finely grated parmesan cheese
¼ teaspoon finely ground black pepper
1 teaspoon dried oregano

1 Combine ingredients in medium bowl. Place 2 teaspoons of mixture, 3cm apart, on baking parchment lined baking trays; flatten with fingertips.
2 Bake, uncovered, in moderately hot oven 4 minutes; cool on trays.

per serving 1.4g fat; 82kJ (20 cal)
tip Although these crisps make a great snack on their own, you can also use them to accompany dips or soup. Make crisps in two large sheets, then break into shards to serve. The flavourings can be omitted and the plain crisps topped with olive paste and a little soured cream for finger food.

olives in cheese pastry

preparation time 35 minutes (plus refrigeration time) **cooking time** 20 minutes **makes** 50

1 cup (150g) plain flour
100g butter, chopped coarsely
1 cup (80g) finely grated parmesan cheese
2 teaspoons dried oregano
2 tablespoons water
50 small stuffed olives

1 Sift flour into a medium bowl; rub in butter. Stir in cheese and oregano; add enough of the water to form soft dough. Cover; refrigerate 30 minutes.
2 Drain olives on absorbent paper. Roll pastry between sheets of baking parchment until 3mm thick; cut 4cm rounds from pastry. Top each round with an olive; fold pastry around olive to enclose.
3 Place 1cm apart on greased baking trays. Cover; refrigerate 30 minutes.
5 Bake in moderately hot oven about 20 minutes until golden; cool.

per pastry 3.2g fat; 157kJ

rocket & parmesan salad

preparation time 25 minutes **cooking time** 3 minutes
serves 8

60g parmesan cheese
200g rocket leaves
80g semi-dried tomatoes, halved lengthways
¼ cup pine nuts (40g), toasted
¼ cup (60ml) balsamic vinegar
¼ cup (60ml) extra virgin olive oil

1 Using vegetable peeler, shave cheese into wide, long pieces.
2 Combine rocket with tomato and nuts in large bowl; add
cheese. Drizzle with combined vinegar and oil; toss gently.

per serving 16g fat; 744kJ (178 cal)
tips Baby spinach can be substituted for rocket. To keep rocket
crisp, rinse under cold water; place in airtight plastic bag and
refrigerate several hours or overnight.
Nuts of any kind can be toasted on top of stove in a dry heavy-
based frying pan, stirring, over medium heat, until they are just
golden brown.

herbed baked ricotta

preparation time 15 minutes **cooking time** 1 hour (plus cooling time)
serves 8

1kg ricotta cheese
2 tablespoons finely chopped fresh thyme
2 cloves garlic, crushed
2 eggs, beaten lightly
1 tablespoon finely chopped garlic chives
1 tablespoon finely grated lemon rind

1 Grease deep 20cm-round cake tin; line base with baking parchment.
2 Place cheese in large bowl with thyme, garlic, eggs, chives and rind;
stir until well combined. Spoon cheese mixture into prepared tin.
3 Bake, uncovered, in moderate oven about 1 hour or until browned lightly
and firm to touch; cool in pan.

per serving 35.7g fat; 1943kJ (464 cal)
tip Try adding a few tablespoons of finely chopped pancetta or black olives
to ricotta mixture before baking.

cheesy antipasti on a stick

preparation time 40 minutes (plus cooling time) **cooking time** 30 minutes
makes 36

6 medium red peppers (1.2kg)
200g ricotta
50g rocket leaves, trimmed, shredded finely
2 drained anchovy fillets, chopped finely
50g marinated artichoke hearts, chopped finely
½ teaspoon dried chilli flakes
36 stuffed large green olives (300g)

1 Cut peppers into sixths lengthways; discard seeds and membranes.
Roast under grill, skin-side up, until skin blisters and blackens. Cover with
plastic or paper for 5 minutes; peel away skin, cool to room temperature.
2 Combine ricotta, rocket, anchovy, artichoke and chilli in bowl. Flatten
pepper pieces; place teaspoons of cheese mixture in centre of each piece
then roll tightly to enclose filling. Thread a roll and an olive onto each skewer.

per skewer 0.8g fat; 105kJ (25 cal)

cheese pasties with tomato sauce

preparation time 50 minutes (plus refrigeration time) **cooking time** 35 minutes
serves 4

1½ cups (240g) wholemeal plain flour
½ cup (75g) plain flour
½ cup (75g) self-raising flour
185g butter
2 teaspoons lemon juice
¼ cup (60ml) water, approximately

ricotta filling
¾ cup (150g) ricotta cheese
¼ cup (20g) grated parmesan cheese
1 egg, beaten lightly
1 medium tomato (190g), chopped finely

60g button mushrooms, sliced thinly
1 teaspoon finely chopped basil
2 tablespoons finely chopped parsley

tomato sauce
15g butter
1 brown onion (150g), chopped finely
1 clove garlic, crushed
425g can tomatoes
200g button mushrooms, sliced thinly
2 teaspoons raw sugar
1 tablespoon finely chopped basil

1 Process flours and butter until just crumbly; gradually stir in juice and enough
of the water to mix to a firm dough.
2 Knead dough on floured surface until smooth; cover with cling film. Refrigerate
30 minutes.
3 Roll dough out on floured surface to a 35cm x 45cm rectangle; cut into
12 rounds using 10cm cutter. Place 1 tablespoon of the ricotta filling in centre
of each round. Lightly brush edges with water; press edges together to seal.
4 Place pasties on oiled baking tray; prick top of pasties using fork. Bake,
uncovered, in hot oven, about 25 minutes or until browned lightly. Serve with
tomato sauce.

ricotta filling Combine ingredients in medium bowl.
tomato sauce Heat butter in small saucepan; cook onion and garlic, stirring,
over medium heat about 2 minutes or until onion is soft. Blend or process
undrained tomatoes; add to onion mixture. Stir in mushrooms, sugar and basil;
bring to a boil. Reduce heat; simmer, uncovered, about 5 minutes or until sauce
thickens slightly.

per serving 50.4g fat; 3523kJ (81 cal)

glossary

blue cheese these are mould-treated cheeses mottled with blue veining. Varieties include firm but crumbly Stilton types to mild, creamy cheeses such as blue brie or gorgonzola.

brie smooth and voluptuous, brie is a French cheese with a bloomy white rind and a creamy centre which becomes runnier as it ripens.

camembert is a soft, creamy French cheese which is made from unpasteurized cow's milk and is ripened for at least three weeks. When fresh, it has a firm, crumbly texture but it ripens and becomes more runny and strongly flavoured as it ripens.

cheddar the most widely eaten cheese in the world, cheddar is a semi-hard cow's milk cheese. It ranges in colour from white to pale yellow and has a slightly crumbly texture and strong flavour if properly matured.

cottage cheese is fresh, white, unripened curd cheese with a grainy consistency. Cottage cheese is low in fat and carbohydrates while high in protein.

cream cheese commonly known as 'Philadelphia', a soft milk cheese having no less than 33 per cent butterfat.

feta a white cheese with milky, fresh acidity. Most commonly made from cow's milk, though sheep and goat's milk varieties are available. Feta is sometimes described as a pickled cheese because it is matured in brine for at least a month, which imparts a strong salty flavour. Feta is solid but crumbles readily.

goat's cheese made from goat's milk, goat's cheese has an earthy, strong taste. It can be purchased in both soft and firm textures, in various shapes and sizes, sometimes rolled in ash or herbs and is available from most supermarkets and delicatessens.

gorgonzola a creamy Italian blue cheese with a mild, sweet taste. Gorgonzola is as good an accompaniment to fruit as it is when used in cooking. Available from most supermarkets and delicatessens.

gruyère a firm, cow's milk Swiss cheese which has small holes and a nutty, slightly salty flavour. Emmental or appenzeller can be used as a substitute. Available from most supermarkets and delicatessens.

haloumi a firm, cream-coloured sheep's milk cheese matured in brine. It has a minty, salty feta-like flavour and can be grilled or fried, briefly, without breaking down. It is available from most supermarkets and Middle-Eastern food stores.

mascarpone is a cultured cream product. Whitish to creamy yellow in colour, it has a soft, creamy texture, a fat content of 75%, and a slightly tangy taste.

mozzarella is an Italian soft, elastic cheese, stretching into long strands when heated. It is used most often on pizzas, but can also be sliced and included in salads, or toasted in cheese sandwiches. It is traditionally made from buffalo milk, but it is now often made from cow's milk. Traditional buffalo mozzarella (*mozzarella di bufala*) can be found in specialty cheese shops and some supermarkets.

parmesan there are two types of Italian parmesan: Parmigiano Reggiano and Parmigiano Pedano. Reggiano is usually aged for three years, giving it a harder texture and a stronger, more mature flavour than Pedano. It also tends to be cheaper and more readily available. Parmesan is best bought in a block, and grated as required, as pre-grated parmesan quickly loses its flavour.

pecorino is the generic Italian name for cheeses made from sheep's milk. It is a hard, white to pale yellow cheese, usually matured for 8 to 12 months. If unavailable, use parmesan.

ricotta a soft white cow's milk cheese. The name roughly translates as 'cooked again' and the cheese is made from whey, a by-product of other cheese making, to which fresh milk and acid are added. Ricotta is a sweet, moist cheese with a fat content of around 8.5% and a slightly grainy texture.

conversion charts

MEASURES

The cup and spoon measurements used in this book are metric: one measuring cup holds approximately 250ml; one metric tablespoon holds 20ml; one metric teaspoon holds 5ml.

All cup and spoon measurements are level.

The most accurate way of measuring dry ingredients is to weigh them. When measuring liquids, use a clear glass or plastic jug with metric markings.

We use large eggs with an average weight of 60g.

warning This book contains recipes for dishes made with raw or lightly cooked eggs. These should be avoided by vulnerable people such as pregnant and nursing mothers, invalids, the elderly, babies and young children.

DRY MEASURES

METRIC	IMPERIAL
15g	½oz
30g	1oz
60g	2oz
90g	3oz
125g	4oz (¼lb)
155g	5oz
185g	6oz
220g	7oz
250g	8oz (½lb)
280g	9oz
315g	10oz
345g	11oz
375g	12oz (¾lb)
410g	13oz
440g	14oz
470g	15oz
500g	16oz (1lb)
750g	24oz (1½lb)
1kg	32oz (2lb)

LIQUID MEASURES

METRIC	IMPERIAL
30ml	1 fl oz
60ml	2 fl oz
100ml	3 fl oz
125ml	4 fl oz
150ml	5 fl oz (¼ pint/1 gill)
190ml	6 fl oz
250ml	8 fl oz
300ml	10 fl oz (½ pint)
500ml	16 fl oz
600ml	20 fl oz (1 pint)
1000ml (1 litre)	1¾ pints

LENGTH MEASURES

METRIC	IMPERIAL
3mm	⅛in
6mm	¼in
1cm	½in
2cm	¾in
2.5cm	1in
5cm	2in
6cm	2½in
8cm	3in
10cm	4in
13cm	5in
15cm	6in
18cm	7in
20cm	8in
23cm	9in
25cm	10in
28cm	11in
30cm	12in (1ft)

OVEN TEMPERATURES

These oven temperatures are only a guide for conventional ovens.
For fan-assisted ovens, check the manufacturer's manual.

	°C (CELSIUS)	°F (FAHRENHEIT)	GAS MARK
Very low	120	250	½
Low	150	275–300	1–2
Moderately low	160	325	3
Moderate	180	350–375	4–5
Moderately hot	200	400	6
Hot	220	425–450	7–8
Very hot	240	475	9

index